Multiple Dog Households

MIRIAM FIELDS-BABINEAU

Contents

Photographers: Miriam Fields-Babineau, Isabelle Francais, Honey Loring, Alice Pantfoeder, Robert Pearcy, Robert Smith, Judith Strom.

© T.F.H. Publications, Inc.

Distributed in the UNITED STATES to the Pet Trade by T.F.H. Publications, Inc., 1 TFH Plaza, Neptune City, NJ 07753; on the Internet at www.tfh.com; in CANADA by Rolf C. Hagen Inc., 3225 Sartelon St., Montreal, Quebec H4R 1E8; Pet Trade by H & L Pet Supplies Inc., 27 Kingston Crescent, Kitchener, Ontario N2B 2T6; in ENGLAND by T.F.H. Publications, PO Box 74, Havant PO9 5TT; in AUSTRALIA AND THE SOUTH PACIFIC by T.F.H. (Australia), Pty. Ltd., Box 149, Brookvale 2100 N.S.W., Australia; in NEW ZEALAND by Brooklands Aquarium Ltd., 5 McGiven Drive, New Plymouth, RD1 New Zealand; in SOUTH AFRICA by Rolf C. Hagen S.A. (PTY.) LTD., P.O. Box 201199, Durban North 4016, South Africa; in JAPAN by T.F.H. Publications. Published by T.F.H. Publications, Inc.

MANUFACTURED IN THE
UNITED STATES OF AMERICA
BY T.F.H. PUBLICATIONS, INC.

More Than One

Just as we humans enjoy each other's company, our canine friends also have a desire to be social. Similar to our desire to spend time with others of our own species, dogs wish to share their lives with a familiar friend. Humans can only do so much. It's rare that we would enjoy a rough game of bite and run, and sniffing behinds is just not in our repertoire.

Dogs need other dogs. This is especially true in households where people work long hours and their beloved canines are left alone all day, every day. This is not a happy life for a dog. Dogs are pack animals and need to feel the closeness of other pack members. Canines learn a lot from each other, such as socialization, problem solving, and reaction to stimuli. These are very important aspects of growing into a well-rounded, properly behaved adult. Just as we obtain dogs for companionship, there are compelling reasons to obtain a companion for your dog. Scruffy will live a happier, more fulfilled life when he has a best friend to share it with.

Besides the obvious need to train both dogs, you will also need to maintain proper pack hierarchy. While you remain in the alpha position, you will need to assert where the rest of the pack lies in the pecking order. This is very important, because if the dogs do not know their positions, there will be fights.

This is often seen when bringing a new dog into the household. The older dog was there first and believes that he should be of a higher position than the new dog. If the new dog tests his own position, the older dog will reassert himself.

Dogs are pack animals and are very comfortable when surrounded by other canines.

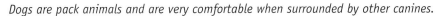

When you introduce a new dog to your household, you must retain the hierarchy and treat your original dog as pack leader.

When bringing home a new dog, it is easiest to introduce a puppy to the family. A puppy will be naturally submissive to an older dog, and the older dog will be more tolerant of a puppy's behavior.

This can be done with as little as a direct stare to as much as a complete display of dominance by mounting, growling, or grabbing the scruff of the neck.

Do not interfere. Granted, you should never allow any dog to show any severely aggressive displays, but, in general, let the dogs decide their positions on their own. Once you interfere, the dogs will become more adamant about solving their position dispute with each other, causing worse fights. Just as people have their likes, dislikes, and opinions, canines have similar emotions. However, there are general ways you can work with the dogs to ease them into a controlled, if not complacent, existence.

There are several ways in which your behavior and reactions can worsen the sibling rivalry. One is to give preferential attention to the new dog, and another is to get in the middle of a spat. Let's say you bring home a cute little puppy. The puppy requires more attention than your well-trained older dog, because you have to go through housetraining and watching the pup constantly

To avoid sibling rivalry and to keep the pack order, always give your original dog attention first.

to make sure he doesn't chew on the wrong things. Your older dog may begin to get jealous and come to you for attention.

Always give dog number one attention first. He deserves it, and it tells him that his place in the hierarchy is safe. Giving the pup preferred attention threatens the older dog's position, and he'll tend to be more aggressive with the pup than he needs to be in order to reassert his position in the pack.

This can be a harder lesson if you bring an adult dog into a home where one already exists, especially if the new dog had been neglected or abused. People tend to coddle the new dog, because he had a tough life before coming to their home and feel that he should receive all their attention and the best of care. Yes, all dogs should receive the best of care, but they should not receive preferred attention. This begins the canine relationship on the wrong paw, because it places the new dog at a higher status than the existing dog, thus causing fights.

Let's say you brought home a two-year-old dog that is skin and bones. You saved him from sure death. Scruffy is happy to have a companion, but notices that you are giving this new dog lots of attention. Scruffy comes up to you for petting, but you ignore him and continue to hug the new dog. Scruffy will go away, but the first chance he's alone with the new dog, he will assert his dominance with growls, snaps, and possibly bites. Had you instead given Scruffy the attention he requested, he would not feel as threatened by the new dog. Admissibly, you should always give your dogs attention on your terms, not on theirs, but never show preferred attention to a dog lower in the hierarchy. This also goes for feeding and training times. The number-one dog gets everything first. This will ensure peace and harmony in a multi-dog household.

Basic obedience training and spaying and neutering will decrease the chances of arguments between your two canine companions.

Begin obedience training with any new dog immediately. As with Scruffy, don't allow the new dog to misbehave at any time, or you'll soon find Scruffy doing the same. This is commonly seen when a new pup arrives and begins messing in the house. Scruffy sees that the new pup is allowed to potty in the house and feels he can do it, too. Not only is this a way to show that he is on equal footing, it's also re-establishing his territory. Dogs

It is hard to pick out just one puppy in a litter, but remember that raising two puppies at once can be very difficult.

naturally urinate over the scent of another dog in their territory. This behavior, however, is usually more prominent with a male dog than with a female dog.

To decrease the possibility of sibling rivalry, make sure all animals are neutered or spayed. It will also help to have dogs of the opposite sex. If you plan on having two male dogs, bring dog number two in as a puppy. This will be less threatening to dog number one. Puppies are allowed many liberties by older dogs. As the pup matures, he'll gradually learn from dog number one what he can and cannot do. These are valuable lessons in socialization and behavior adjustment that are more easily taught by another canine than by a human. Again, unless the older dog is being overly aggressive, don't interfere with the lessons that dog number one is teaching to the pup. In fact, you should watch closely and emulate the behavior to ensure that your puppy understands you better. There is much you can learn from observing your dogs in action.

The only time you should interfere with a hierarchy spat is when dog number one is geriatric. Dog number one may become easily irritated due to discomfort or pain. In the wild, he would be gradually overwhelmed and lowered in the pack order, but due to our love for our cherished old dog, we need to protect him. It would be a good idea to keep him separate from the younger dog when feeding and resting. Keep a close watch on them when they are together. If the younger dog begins to show dominance or aggressive play behavior, quickly separate them. Your older dog has earned some respect, as well as peace and quiet.

If you are one of those people who fell in love with two puppies at the same time and couldn't decide which one to take home, you have some other issues to confront. First of all, although it may be a difficult decision, you really should make up your mind to take just one. Raising two puppies at the same time can be very difficult. Second, you must be certain that you have the time and the financial means to care for them.

Dogs are not creatures you can stick in a cage and forget about until feeding time. They require your every free moment for guidance, nurture, and care. With two puppies, you are going to have to deal with essentially two babies that will need diaper changes (being let outside), feeding, "babysitting" to ensure that nothing dangerous is consumed or destroyed, veterinary care, grooming, and more. In essence, you will need to be able to spend the entire day with them and find someone to fill in for you when you can't be there.

These are some of the obstacles you'll need to deal with, whether you get two puppies at the same time or simply have two dogs.

FEEDING REQUIREMENTS

If the dogs have different dietary requirements, you will have to obtain the different

Puppies are always hungry and are notoriously greedy around feeding time. If stealing or food guarding occurs, feed them separately in their crates.

Keep an eye on your dogs during feeding time to ensure that they are both getting the proper nutrition.

foods and watch over them during feeding time to make sure they eat their own food.

Puppies are notorious for always wanting what the other pup has. It's common for them to switch from bowl to bowl until the food is consumed. If one of your pups has a medical condition that requires special food, you must separate them during feeding, which can easily be done by feeding them in their crates. Not only can you more easily monitor how much they consume, but they also learn that their crates are nice places to be.

FINANCIAL COMMITMENT

With two or more dogs in your house, your veterinary bill will be twice (or three times) as much. They must receive their initial puppy vaccines that are given every two weeks for six weeks, then the rabies vaccine when they reach four months, as well as yearly boosters, monthly flea and heartworm preventative, medications for infections or injuries, and more. As the dogs age, there are geriatric conditions that will require veterinary attention.

If you have the types of dog that require special grooming, such as Poodles, terriers, or spaniels, there is the cost of regular trips to the groomer to consider. Even if you choose to bathe and clip your pups yourself, you'll use more shampoo and other grooming equipment.

Two or more dogs means double or triple the responsibility and expenses—make sure you are prepared to provide all the dogs in your household with the proper care and attention.

The cost of food will double. It may not cost much to feed two Pomeranians, but imagine the cost of feeding two Great Danes. If you insist on having two puppies at once, be sure to consider the size of dogs that you can afford and have room for.

Kenneling when you go out of town is also an issue. While this is a good reason to have two dogs, because they will keep each other company, you will also have the increased cost of boarding two versus one. You may want to research the kennels in your area and make sure the one that you choose will allow your dogs to remain together. Often, there is a reduced rate for using one run for two dogs.

TIME COMMITMENT

Not only will it take more time to buy supplies, feed your dogs, and take them to the veterinarian, you will also need to train and exercise them. Two puppies will be more difficult to handle, because they will need to be housetrained and must go through their initial obedience training and practice separately. However, once you have two well-trained dogs, your time commitment will be reduced.

When your second dog initially comes into your home, you will need to spend a lot of time helping the two dogs

Consider the size of both of your dogs as adults before taking them home. These two Great Danes will need plenty of room to exercise and plenty of food to stay healthy.

Owning more than one dog will require a great deal of your time and energy, but the benefits can be great for you and for the dogs.

adjust. A new puppy will be more easily accepted, but there's still the time commitment of housetraining and conditioning the new addition. Bringing home an older dog may require special handling when being introduced to the existing canine resident. This can take anywhere from a few hours to weeks. It all depends on the dog's individual personality.

There are those of us who wish to live with more than two dogs. Our family is not complete without three or more canine friends. Having a lot of dogs is not difficult, providing all are well trained and socialized. If you have the financial means and the time to spend with all your canine friends, life can be harmonious. Many dog breeders will keep multiple breeding stock for their programs. Dog lovers will save as many dogs from abuse or certain death as they possibly can. Trainers like having a number of dogs to compete with. The distinction of these situations is that these people have the time and facilities in which to keep more than two dogs. More than two dogs living in a home without the indoor space and fenced-in outdoor exercise areas can make this a difficult situation. Neighbors are bound to complain of noise and smell. The dogs can become destructive if not properly trained and contained. You should not have more than two dogs if you don't have the time, money, and proper facility in which to keep them. Yes, many of us simply want to save as many homeless dogs as we can, but this can backfire on you if they ultimately do not receive the care they require.

While having more than one dog requires much more from you, the benefits far outweigh the complications. In essence, you are giving your dog a friend and companion with which he can identify and bond. You are also giving yourself the unconditional love of another dog, which is priceless.

If all of the dogs in your household are well trained and socialized, it will not be difficult to maintain a big, happy family.

Introducing Your Dogs

How your dogs behave during their introduction depends mostly on you. First of all, you should make sure that the second dog is extremely friendly and/or submissive, of the opposite sex, or a puppy. Any of these factors can ensure a quicker, less troublesome introduction. Well-socialized dogs will often be far more accepting of new dogs than a dog that has lived alone without playmates for many years.

Puppies are usually easily accepted by older dogs, regardless of age or sex, because they are not seen as a territorial threat. Their antics are tolerated until they reach adolescence, at which time they are quickly taught social order by the older dog. The puppy will emulate the other dog's behavior and learn both the good and bad habits of his adopted sibling.

Bringing home a dog of the opposite sex is also less threatening to an existing dog than one of the same sex, especially if the dogs are not neutered. In a wild dog pack, there are two hierarchical factions. One consists of the male dogs and the other of the female dogs. With dogs of the opposite sex, there are

Well-socialized dogs that have been around other canines since puppyhood will have little trouble accepting another dog into the family.

Usually, older dogs are more willing to accept a puppy into the home; however, the puppy will most likely emulate the behaviors, both good and bad, of the older dog.

rarely conflicts, due to the female and male switching their dominance patterns. For example, the male may show dominance when dealing with territory, and the female may show dominance around a special toy or food. These are common behaviors in wild canines—the males protect their territories by scent marking and patrolling, while the females are in charge of feeding the brood. Thus, male and female

Pick a neutral place, such as a park, to introduce your dogs to each other. This way, there will be less fighting over territory.

dogs will tend to get along better than those of the same sex. There are many exceptions to these statements, however, and the final result depends on each individual's personality.

If you plan on introducing an older dog to your existing companion, you'll want to be sure that he has a submissive temperament. This way, he will immediately defer to your existing dog and will be less threatening to his pack position. The decreased threat will increase acceptance.

The real disasters happen when you introduce a dominant or adolescent dog to a home where your other dog has ruled his domain. This is especially dangerous if your dog controls you and the household as well. It would be wise to make sure your existing dog has completed obedience training and has no bad habits before bringing home another dog. A trained dog will be far easier to control, because he knows that you have the ultimate say in how he is allowed to behave.

No matter how well-socialized puppies may be, there will always be some struggling for the position of top dog. If you allow them to work it out themselves, they will be less likely to fight when older.

Regardless of sex, most dogs are territorial. Some will bark at intruders; others will charge an intruder. In your dog's eyes, another dog on the property constitutes an intruder. The natural reaction is to reassert territorial rights and run off the interloper.

When your dogs first meet, try practicing obedience commands. It can be very useful in reminding your dogs that you are the leader of the pack.

For a highly territorial dog, meeting another dog for the first time on his home ground can cause anxiety, followed by possible aggression. It's always a good idea for the dogs to meet for the first time in neutral territory.

If you are getting your new dog from a shelter or rescue group, bring your existing companion to the location or somewhere nearby so that the two dogs can meet. Meeting on neutral ground will prevent territorial aggression, and you'll get a better idea of how the two dogs will get along when the actual "pack merging" takes place. Your dogs will first sniff noses, then smell the anal area. There may be a moment or two of hierarchical challenge, such as a paw over the back or a game of tag. One dog may mount the other. This is a sign of dominance, not a sexual display (unless, of course, you're letting an intact male meet a female in season).

If you don't have the luxury of utilizing a neutral area near the new dog's location, take both dogs to a nearby park or common area. Many dogs visit these areas, so dog number one may not exhibit territorial claims, leaving him more amenable to the new dog.

When allowing the dogs to meet for the first time, keep the leashes loose and remain calm. If you see any aggressive displays, such as placing a paw on the back, mounting, or snarling, immediately get the dogs involved in some other activity. Throwing a ball or telling them to come can take their minds off of showing dominance. Above all, remain calm. The dogs will immediately sense any tension on your part. If your dog does not listen to you, make him. Be consistent, regardless of this new situation, and your dog will learn that there is nothing to be nervous about.

If both dogs are trained, you can gradually acclimate them through first working them in the same vicinity. Put them through their obedience behaviors; have them heel alongside each other or perform a sit or down/stay side by side. This keeps the entire meeting under your control, never allowing the dogs to display anything other than attention to their handler. When they learn to work near each other, you can allow them some time to touch noses and, finally, to play together.

MULTIPLE DOG HOUSEHOLDS

Above: *When making introductions, remain calm and try to divert any aggressive displays with activities that both dogs can participate in.*

Below: *It will take patience and time in the beginning, but owning two dogs eventually can be a pleasure for the whole family.*

Housetraining and Behavior Modification Times Two

Bringing another dog into your home can often upset the balance of power—hierarchical power, that is. An existing dog has learned his place in your family pack, but the new dog, especially a youngster, may come into your home and misbehave, causing your other dog to also display some bad behavior. Then again, a new dog will also learn bad habits from the existing dog, such as getting into the garbage, barking excessively, or jumping on furniture.

While the dogs are determining their pack positions, they may also challenge your alpha position. You may tell your older dog to sit or lie down and he will choose to ignore you because of the presence of the other dog. While in one sense, the other dog represents a simple distraction, in another it is a direct challenge of your authority. All your dogs must listen to your commands, regardless of each other's presence.

All your dogs must be taught the house rules, which, if you want a harmonious pack, should consist of the following:

Any new dogs in your household will pick up the habits of your original dog. It is important that your first dog be well trained before adding another to the home.

Providing your dogs with lots of chew toys, especially if they are puppies, will save your belongings and keep your dogs safe.

1. No jumping—especially on people, counter tops, or furniture. This is especially important in a home with children or elderly residents. Even if your dog is small, this is a good rule to follow. Jumping up is a form of domination. Each time your dog jumps on your legs, he is telling you what to do; namely, "Pick me up," or "Give me attention." If one of your dogs is big and the other is small, you should most definitely not allow the small one to jump up while punishing the large dog for it. If the larger dog was your first dog, it may cause some sibling rivalry problems. Forbidding counter top jumping is self-explanatory. When you leave your Thanksgiving turkey and pumpkin pie on the counter to cool, would you rather see you or your dogs enjoying dinner?

Be sure to institute some basic household rules that apply to all the animals in your family and be consistent when enforcing them.

2. No chewing anything other than dog toys. No dog, regardless of size or age, should put his mouth on anything other than toys allotted to canine play. Make sure that there are plenty of toys to go around for all the dogs. In fact, you may want to have two of the same type available. Don't let an old shoe or towel become part of your dog's possessions—then newer shoes, socks, and towels will be fair game as well.

Begging for food can be an annoying habit, especially if there is more than one dog staring at you while you eat. Never feed your dogs from the table and only give them nutritious treats.

3. Stay out of the garbage. You can either put the garbage in a cupboard or teach the dogs to leave it alone. If you are strapped for time, put the garbage can in an area that is out of the reach of your dogs. In fact, if you are throwing away food or something else that is very enticing, be sure to empty the garbage as quickly as possible to prevent your dogs from giving in to their strong food drives. If you wish to leave the garbage in a convenient area, you will have to train your dogs to ignore the can.

4. Do not bark excessively. One or two barks are allowed when someone comes to your door, but barking at everyone who passes by your home, including dogs, cats, squirrels, and butterflies, should not be allowed. Running the fence and barking at the neighbor's dog can be annoying, and barking for attention is a definite no-no. Barking when playing with siblings can become out of hand as well, so keep that to a minimum, especially if you have close neighbors.

5. No begging. Not only is this an annoying habit, but it also can be very unhealthy for your dog if people give in to it. Dogs need to have their diets strictly monitored. This is especially important for a dog that has any physical dysfunction, is overweight, or is within a specialized age group, such as an elderly dog or a puppy. Dogs should receive all of their food in their own dishes or from your hand when you are offering a special treat for performing a good behavior.

Offer your dogs treats and safe toys as rewards for good behavior. Positive motivation will keep them out of trouble.

Each dog that resides in your home should have his own private space to which he can retreat and relax. Crates are ideal for providing them with somewhere to call home.

6. Your dogs should receive praise and treats only when performing good behavior. Don't give them a treat simply for being there. Dogs have the desire to do something with their lives. Giving them a job, such as sitting or staying before receiving praise, offers them an outlet and something to look forward to. Offering them a reward for being good dogs during the day while you were away at work should still coincide with doing a sit or another behavior first, because the dogs will not connect their good behavior with the reward.

7. Each dog should have their own space, whether it is a crate or bed. This allows for all of the dogs to feel like "king" of their little domain. Every dog needs a place to retreat when tired of the household activities. Make sure that young children do not invade these territories. While most dogs will accept them, other dogs, especially those that are stressed, may become aggressive.

HOUSETRAINING

Housetraining two dogs simultaneously is extremely difficult, especially if both are young puppies. If you have fallen into this situation, you must be sure to contain them in separate crates or pens when you cannot watch them and keep a constant vigil when you are with them. When young puppies are out of their containment areas, they should remain in one part of your home, such as the kitchen, where the flooring allows for easy clean up. Stay with them and watch for the telltale signs of having to go potty, such as circling or sniffing. Two puppies playing together will have to go potty more often, because their high activity increases their metabolism rates. In general, puppies need to go potty after napping, eating, drinking, and playing.

Dogs will display obvious signs that they need to go out to eliminate, like sniffing and circling. In order to facilitate the housebreaking process, it is important to get them outside as soon as possible.

Neither rain, sleet, nor snow should prevent you from taking your dogs for daily walks. Outside time gives them a chance to eliminate and exercise.

If you take your puppies to a relief area directly after these events, you'll have an easier time with housetraining. You can increase the speed of housetraining by teaching them to go potty on command. Any puppy eight weeks of age or older can learn this behavior within a week, provided you are consistent. With two puppies, it is a godsend. Follow these steps:

1. Take your puppies outside as soon as they wake up in the morning. You may want to carry them to their relief area. If you're dealing with a large breed, walk them quickly.

2. As soon as they reach their relief area, give them a potty command, such as Hurry, Potty, Business, or something else that is not offensive to those who may be listening. Continue saying it over and over until each puppy relieves himself.

3. When one of the puppies goes, give him praise and a treat. Continue to encourage the other puppy. When the second puppy goes, give him praise and a treat as well. After they are through, allow the puppies to play outside for a few minutes. When you bring them indoors, allow them to remain in your kitchen or other "puppy-proofed" area of your home for a half hour to 45 minutes.

Repeat this exercise within 15 minutes after eating, directly after a nap, and every hour during the day if the puppies are playing together. Take them outside through the same door each time so that they learn the path to their relief area. Once a pup learns the routine, they often go to the door to let you know they have to go potty.

If you find that your puppies are too distracted by each other to relieve themselves when and where they are supposed to, then you will need to take them out separately. You can still utilize the same go-on-command training

You can teach your dogs to perform certain commands to let you know when they need to go out. These two English Springer Spaniels wait patiently to be let back in.

methods. The puppy that remains indoors while you are walking should be contained to stay out of trouble.

Many people wish that their dogs would tell them when they have to go potty. However, without the means of using human speech, the dogs either have to bark, scratch the door, or perform some other annoying behavior that is often punished, thus defeating the purpose. Instead, teach your dog to ring a bell when he needs to go outside. This adds both stimulation and enjoyment to housetraining.

Hang a cow bell from the knob of the door leading to your dog's relief area. Each time you let your dog out, smear some cheese on the bell. Show your dog the cheese and allow him to lick it. As he licks the bell, it will ring. As soon as the bell makes noise, open the door and take your dog to his relief area. Use your "potty word" over and over until he relieves himself, then give your dog praise and a treat. Within a week, your dog (or puppy) will learn to ring the bell to go outside. This is a great trick to teach your older dog, too—every dog enjoys learning new things.

PROBLEM BEHAVIOR

Destructive Chewing

While your dogs will usually choose to play together instead of destroying your furniture, puppies will often take something with which to play tug-of-war. This object can be either a pull toy or a couch cushion. It is your job to ensure that your dogs know what they can and cannot play with.

You can begin the training lessons by always being present when your dogs are loose in your home or garden. However, while you can usually control the objects

Safe chew toys will keep your puppies' teeth and gums healthy and can be used as rewards in training exercises.

that they play with in your home, it is far more difficult to do so in your yard, unless you intend to be there at all times while your dogs are outside. It might be a good idea to fence off an area where you do not have any landscaping and make a place where the dogs can dig, roll, and run.

At the first sign of your dog's interest in a particular household item, be sure to say, "No!" in a low, growly tone of voice and push him away. Pick up one of your dog's toys and offer him that. Play with the toy and your dogs at the same time. This makes the game more interesting. Offering your dogs your attention only when they do bad things will encourage them to continue, because they may think that it is far better to get negative attention than none at all.

Another way to keep your dogs interested in the toys is to rotate them. Offer different toys every other day. There are some toys that can be reused in different ways, making them more fun. A Kong toy, for example, can be filled with biscuits or kibble. A shank bone can also be filled with enticing treats. A Buster Cube can be filled with kibble and your dogs can roll it around, gathering the kibble as it falls out. A stimulated dog will rarely become destructive.

When you cannot be with your dogs, they need to be contained in a safe, dog-proofed area where they will remain out of trouble. This not only teaches them proper behavior in the rest of your home, it also offers them a feeling of safety, both physically and mentally. Dogs love having their own "dens," which a crate or fenced-off room gives to them. Making this part of your dogs' routine will ensure a harmonious relationship for everybody. Allowing your dog access to the entire house while you are gone can be very dangerous. There are many things in your home that can cause serious injury, such as foam from cushions, stockings, detergents, and garbage. Even some of the best-trained dogs will get into trouble every so often. You don't want to take that chance with your beloved companions.

Dogs will often get into fights over possessions like toys, so make sure you have enough on hand for everyone.

Every dog in your household needs to know that they must obey the rules. If you allow one dog to get away with something, like sleeping on the bed, the other dog is sure to follow.

Jumping Up

If Scruffy weighs over two pounds, his jumping up can be annoying. Not only is it a means of garnering attention, it is also a canine manner of domination. At first, your dog may jump up on you to greet you. When he learns that this gets him attention, he will begin jumping on you more and more. He is now dominating you by demanding attention instead of waiting for you to offer it. Whether you own small or large dogs, jumping up should not be allowed.

You can often prevent the bad behavior by offering a proper canine greeting when you come home. Dogs first greet each other by touching noses and sniffing rears. This offers them an opportunity to learn about their new friend through body and chemical language, the most utilized forms of canine communication. Crouching down to greet Scruffy will offer him a chance to touch your nose, lick your face, or, if he's very large, knock you over with enthusiasm, and he won't have to jump up to do so. When you own more than one dog and they all greet you at the same time, it can be utter chaos. The problem will not be isolated to having a bunch of paws and licking muzzles coming at you. It may cause scuffles between the dogs as they vie to be the first dog to receive your greeting.

If you choose not to greet your dogs in this manner, Scruffy and his pals can learn to change their habits and sit when you greet them. This is a controlled means of greeting and far more pleasant for most humans, because it can be difficult to crouch down and most of us would like to avoid being bowled over by large, enthusiastic dogs. Through patience, persistence, and consistency, your dogs will learn to eagerly sit for attention.

Even small dogs can overwhelm you when they all greet you at once. Teaching basic obedience commands can help you to control their enthusiasm.

Begin this lesson by always making your dogs sit before they receive any petting or food. Each time they either enter or exit your home or a gate of any type, make them sit. Make sure you are consistent with these procedures, or the dogs will continue to jump on you.

As soon as possible, change your own habits. Don't allow your dog to jump on you at any given time. There are several ways to handle this. If your dog is under 15 pounds or is a puppy under 4 months of age, you can do one of two things: Push Scruffy away as you say, "Scruffy, No!"; or as Scruffy jumps up, step backward and say, "Scruffy, Sit!" in a demanding tone of voice. Be certain to make him sit if he does not do so. As soon as Scruffy stops jumping up and is in a sitting position, praise him.

For larger dogs, the best way to keep them from jumping on you, the furniture, the counter tops, and your guests is to use a noise box. The noise box should be a metal can, such as a small paint can or bandage box. Don't use an aluminum can, because the sound may not be effective. Put 15 pennies in a few cans and cover them securely. Place the cans in areas where your dogs are most likely to jump up, such as near the doors, in the family room, and in the kitchen. Each time your dogs jump up, shake the can in a hard, up-and-down motion once or twice as you say, "No!" in a low, growly tone of voice. The effects will be immediate. The sound coupled with your reprimand should startle them enough to make them get down. As soon as the dogs have all four paws on the

Dogs jump up as a way to show their affection. With more than one dog in the house, however, it is best to teach them to sit for attention and praise.

Two dogs can get into double the trouble, which is why it is important to curb problem behaviors from the very beginning.

ground, tell them to sit. Always praise them when they respond. If they do not do as you asked, make them. Sometimes you have to show your dogs what you are talking about in order for the message to get through; however, losing your temper is the last thing you should do. Remain calm and in control and the problem will be solved. Keep that can handy!

Excessive Barking

In a household with more than one barking dog, the chorus can be-

Good manners are important for every dog to have in order to become a valued member of the family.

come annoying, especially to neighbors. Often, a new dog will pick up this habit from the first dog. While many people own dogs for the purpose of home security, the last thing they want is for their dogs to bark at friends, neighbors, and squirrels. Barking at the occasional solicitor is fine, barking at an intruder is fine, but the howling simply must be controlled.

Your dogs should learn a "shut-off" word, such as Enough, Quiet, or Stop. With more than one dog barking, this can be difficult to teach, so it's best to begin be-

With more than one hungry puppy around, mealtime can become chaotic. It is important to teach your dogs to sit and wait for every meal.

havior modification with the instigator of the chorus line. The best means of making sure that you can back up your correction is to have leashes on your dogs. You may want to use three- or four-foot leashes for this purpose so that there is less chance of them wrapping around furniture.

To stop excessive barking, try the following: When the dog barks, take hold of the leash and say, "Scruffy, Enough!" in a demanding tone of voice. Be sure to look him in the eyes and maintain your hold on him until he looks away and stops making noise. Do this every time he barks excessively. After correcting the instigator, then correct the other dog(s) in the same manner.

To control the barking when someone comes to your door, teach your dogs to perform sit/stays or down/stays. Not only will this control the noise level, it will also keep the dogs from charging the door when you open it. Seeing a well-trained dog doing a sit/stay at the door is normally enough to deter someone with bad intentions, and friends and family can enter your home without being accosted by a wild pack of dogs.

Every dog deserves to be taught the household rules in order to become a good companion.

Begging

This bad habit begins with you or someone in your family giving your dogs a piece of human food. Whether you do this at the table, standing at the kitchen counter, or sitting on the sofa does not make a difference. You are essentially teaching your dogs that if they sit and stare at you while you eat, they will be rewarded.

If it is already too late and your dogs beg while you are eating, you can correct the problem in one of the following ways, depending on the "pushiness" of your dog(s). If you have a really adamant dog that jumps on you or shoves his nose in your lap, push him away firmly as you say, "No!" in a low, growly tone of voice. If your dog sits and stares at you, send him to his bed and put him in a down/stay. Another means of taking your dogs' minds off of your evening meal is to offer them an enticing toy, such as a Buster Cube or a treat-filled Kong toy. If none of the above-mentioned modifications work, you will have to put your dogs in a crate or fenced-off area while you eat. Do not, however, do this first, because it does not cure the problem—it only avoids the confrontation.

Some dogs, like Beagles, are predisposed to barking. Having a companion can often reduce the incidence of barking because of boredom or loneliness.

You may have many other types of behavior problems to deal with, especially if one or more of your dogs were over the age of six months when you obtained them. By this age, they have figured out where they stand among their pack and are far more difficult to retrain. If you are faced with more difficult problems, such as aggression, it would be a good idea to hire a behaviorist or trainer.

Making time to spend with each dog individually will help you to strengthen the bond between dog and owner.

Care and Feeding

Each of your dogs is an individual and has special needs. These needs must be addressed daily in order to maintain control of your mini-pack. An older dog may need medication and a thorough body checkup. A younger dog may need to release some energy through playing fetch. Regardless of the need, make the time for each dog. This is very important for bonding. You want your dog to give you the utmost respect and love. This individual time together will promote those emotions.

Feeding time can often be a challenge. Each dog will want what the other dog has, regardless of what it is. If you can keep all your dogs on the same diet, this may not present a problem, but as dogs age, they tend to require special diets. Also, some dogs eat slower than others, although you'll discover that the more dogs you have, the faster they'll eat, competing with each other.

In order to ensure that your dogs eat what they must, you may need to separate them during feeding time. You can do this easily by putting them in crates or placing their dishes on opposite sides of a room with you

Make sure you give each dog in your household a dog food that is made for their stage of life.

Monitor how much and how quickly each dog eats in order to prevent bloat and other gastrointestinal problems.

standing in between. Eating too quickly can present a problem for a dog with a tendency to bloat. You should separate this individual from the rest of the pack to ensure that he eats slower. If this does not stop him from inhaling his food, you'll have to remain with him while he eats, dole out small portions at a time, or feed him smaller portions throughout the day.

Dogs learn behavior patterns very quickly. Eventually, you won't have to be present to ensure that each dog eats his own food. However, if you have a dog that thinks his purpose in life is to eat anything, regardless of whose food it may be, you should always remain nearby. This is especially important when you have more than one dominant canine or an adolescent dog between the ages of 7 to 18 months.

A word about your dog's diet: Read the labels! There are some processed pet foods that can be detrimental to your dog's health. Additives, preservatives, and other toxins can cause allergic reactions in sensitive or elderly pets. Normally, the first three ingredients are the main part of the food. If the ingredients mentioned are grain or meal, then it is best not to use this food, because you are feeding your dog mostly grain instead of the meat that should make up the main part of his diet. Dogs are mainly carnivorous and it takes a lot of careful nutritional planning for them to lead a healthy existence as vegetarians. Granted, they should have fruits, dairy, and vegetables to maintain proper health, but meat should be the main part of their diet.

If you are using a commercially processed food, you should give your dogs something raw just before you feed them the kibble. A piece of carrot, raw chicken, banana, or broccoli would work nicely. This raw food will allow Scruffy's digestive enzymes to begin their job of metabolizing the food and sending the nutrients to the proper places. A processed food will not initiate these enzymes, because the food is already predigested. In fact, mixing some raw food into the diet will help overall digestion and usage, thus using less food. When you live with more than one dog, cutting down on the cost of food is beneficial, and you'll have less feces to clean up afterward because more of the food is utilized.

It is always a good idea to speak with your veterinarian or a canine nutritionist about which food would best suit your dog's physical condition. An elderly dog will

Every dog in your care should have access to cool, clean water at all times.

require a diet high in fiber and low in carbohydrates and fat, as well as extra supplements, such as glycosamine and chondroitin sulfates for healthy joints. A young dog will require high levels of protein, fat, and carbohydrates for their elevated activity levels. Overweight dogs and those that are not very active need a low-calorie diet.

If one of your dogs suffers from chronic allergies and organ dysfunction, you should consult with a holistic veterinarian for ways of helping your dog's body heal itself. This is far more productive than breaking down his immunity with the repeated use of antibiotics and steroids. Granted, these medications are often needed, but after repeated usage, they lose their potency, because the body's bacteria form a tolerance.

If any one of your dogs suffers from nutritional deficiencies or age-related problems, you should feed them separately to ensure that they are getting the proper nutrition.

GROOMING

A daily body checkup is very important when you live with more than one dog. Dogs tend to play roughly, often causing injury. The injury could be anything from a scratch to a pulled muscle. The sooner you discover something, the less of a negative impact it will have on the dog. This is especially important if an individual of your pack is elderly. They tend to become injured more easily and, due to their advanced age, can contract an illness or allergy. Early detection could save a life.

When doing the daily body check, begin at your dog's head. Rub his forehead, look in his eyes and ears, and check his gums and teeth. If your dog spends any time outdoors during the day, search for ticks in moist areas, such as inside the ears, along the muzzle, along the back (where the parasites drop off vegetation), and under the legs. Work your way down his neck and chest, moving your fingers in a circular motion. This movement not only allows you to cover most of the skin surface but also massages and relaxes your dog. Once you have completed a thorough check of Scruffy's head and neck region, move your hands down his spine, then rub his sides and tummy. If your dog has a tail, save that for last and be extra sensitive, because many dogs do not like their tails being examined.

Once the body check is complete, take your grooming utensils and brush out any mats and knots. Often, debris can become embedded in mats and cause irritation. For

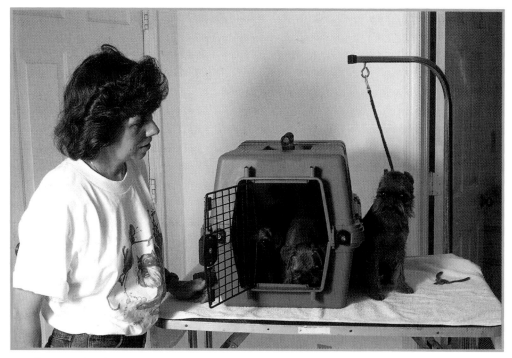

Regular grooming is important to keep your dog's skin and coat looking good and enables you to keep on top of any problems your dogs may experience.

dogs with bulging eyes, such as Pomeranians or Chihuahuas, or with long fur over their eyes, such as Briards or Old English Sheepdogs, apply an eye wash to rinse out mucous and debris. Dogs with droopy ears should have their ears thoroughly cleaned at least once a week. Breeds with folds in their skin like Bulldogs and Shar Peis will need to have those folds gently spread and cleaned. Some dogs will need to have their anal sacs expressed on a regular basis to prevent impaction.

Dogs that have an abundance of hair around their faces, like these Shih Tzu, need extra care to keep their eyes clear and free of debris.

Ear Cleaning

Ear cleaning is essential for overall good health, especially for dogs with ears that fold over or completely flop down, such as retrievers and spaniels. With ears of this type, the air cannot circulate into the canals. This keeps them moist and makes them a breeding ground for yeast and bacteria. Repeated infections can eventually lead to deafness and other neurological problems.

There are several ways to detect an ear infection. First of all, your dog will let you know his ears are bothering him by repeatedly shaking his head. Scruffy may also show sensitivity to being touched on his ear or the surrounding area, and you may smell an unpleasant odor. If any of these symptoms occur, take Scruffy to your veterinarian immediately. The sooner the infection is treated, the less of a chance of permanent injury.

To prevent this from happening, have your veterinarian recommend a specific ear cleanser for your companion. Put a squirt of the cleaner on a soft rag and clean around the outer ear and canal regularly. Do not press the cloth into the canal. This is a very sensitive area and easily injured. If your dog tends to squirm, teach him how to sit and stay while having his ears done. After several applications, Scruffy will learn to remain still, especially if he gets a special treat afterward.

Tooth Care

Caring for your dog's pearly whites is as important as caring for your own. The more you brush his teeth, the longer he will have them and the longer you'll allow him to kiss you. Yes, dogs can still have a full set of teeth when elderly and fresh breath, too! In fact, having healthy teeth will prevent your dog from contracting many illnesses associated with periodontal disease and the inability to chew food properly. Try to brush Scruffy's teeth at least three times per week.

If your dog is not used to having his teeth brushed, begin with a soft cloth wrapped around your forefinger. Apply some warm water and a bit of special dog toothpaste

Regular ear cleaning is necessary to keep your dogs' ears free of infection. Breeds that have long ears, like the Basset Hound, should have their ears checked on a regular basis.

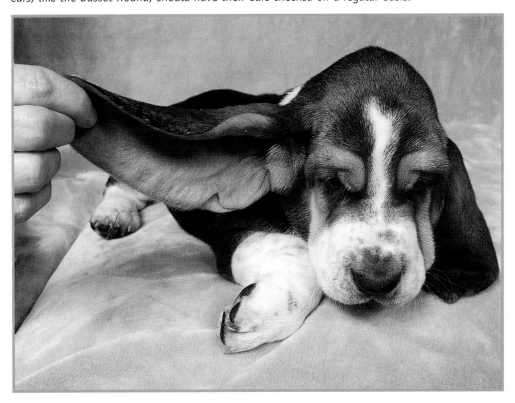

Many breeds need extensive grooming. There are kits available that provide all the equipment you'll need, including clippers, combs, brushes and oil, to keep your dog looking neat and in great shape. Photo courtesy of Wahl Clipper Corp.

with meat flavor to the cloth. It is important to use canine toothpaste, because it does not have any foaming agents, as does human toothpaste. Your dog will not appreciate a mouth full of bubbles and he may swallow the toothpaste, causing stomach problems.

Place your dog in a sit/stay and put your finger into the side of his mouth so that you can begin by cleaning his back teeth. Rub each tooth in a circular manner from his gums to the tip and behind. Work your way toward his front teeth and then around to the other side. When Scruffy is accustomed to having his teeth cleaned, you can use a toothbrush.

Bathing

Indoor dogs need to be bathed about every 10 to 14 days. This will cut down on the hair, dander, and odors associated with having your companions indoors. Dogs that have the opportunity to play together outside should be bathed more often, because they tend to get much dirtier.

Bathing can be done in several ways. The easiest way is to take your companions to a professional groomer, where they will be washed, dried, and clipped. If this represents a financial hardship, then obtain some quality dog shampoo and use

Bath time can be fun if you share it with friends—both canine and human. These Australian Cattle Dogs take a dip with their young owners.

your bathtub or, weather permitting, the garden hose. It is easiest to bathe a dog that is obedience trained. Not only is the bath quicker and more efficient, but you might manage to remain fairly dry.

When bathing a trained dog in the bathtub, you can do the following:

1. Fill the tub with lukewarm water and then have your dog jump in, or if he's nervous, pick him up and place him in.

2. Put a mild ophthalmic solution in his eyes to prevent soap irritation. It would also be

a good idea to put tissue or cotton in his ears to prevent moisture from running inside. Be sure you don't push the tissue or cotton in too deeply.

3. Have your dog do a down/stay while you pour water over his back and head.

4. Once soaked, put your hand under Scruffy's tummy and tell him to do a stand/stay.

5. While he stands, soap him all over, starting with the neck, then the head, followed by his body and legs.

6. Again, put Scruffy in a down/stay while you rinse him all over. The water will tend to become soapy, so run the faucet and place a large cup under for fresh rinsing water.

7. Have Scruffy do another stand/stay while you rinse him all over with the fresh water.

8. Let the water drain, close the shower curtain or doors, and allow Scruffy to shake.

8. Towel dry the dog and/or use a hair dryer on a cool setting.

Now you have a clean dog without your having to get a bath, too—on to the next one!

When bathing your dogs with the outdoor hose, first attach their leashes and have them remain in a stand/stay the entire time. If they try to back away, bring them back to you, gently but firmly. Repeat your stand/stay command.

Puppies can easily be bathed in a deep sink, but it would be a good idea to make sure your pup understands at least some semblance of a sit/stay. Otherwise, the entire experience will be very negative and your pup will wish to avoid bath times instead of jumping right in. An intimidated pup can often learn to accept bath time if he sees one of his older siblings being bathed first. A well-trained role model has the best influence.

A well-groomed dog is a happier dog, so don't let cumbersome grooming tools stop you from getting the job done. There are compact, lightweight tools available. Photo courtesy of Wahl, USA.

Nail Clipping

Your dog's nails need to be clipped every six weeks. If you are at all squeamish or insecure about performing this task, take your dogs to your veterinarian or groomer. It is very important that this is done properly, because a nail that is trimmed too short can cause a lot of bleeding and discomfort.

If you wish to take on this task yourself, have a professional show you how to do it. Take a close look at your dogs' nails. They have a pink, pulpy substance inside, similar to the tissue beneath your nails. The nails curve like a hawk's beak and then form a pointy tip. It is just after this curve that you'll want to clip. If your dog's nails are black, you must be very careful. It would be a good idea to clip at least a quarter inch away from the curve and utilize an electric filer to round and trim a little more.

Many breeds, like these Chesapeake Bay Retrievers, have a natural affinity for water and coats that do not require heavy maintenance.

DAILY SCHEDULE

Caring for two or more dogs can be time-consuming, but if you work them into a daily routine, it won't take much more time than caring for one dog. The first thing you'll need to establish is proper time management. All the dogs will need feeding, grooming, exercise, and training. Working everything into a schedule will be helpful.

Here is a sample schedule for someone who is home during the day with the dogs:

• 6 am: Let the dogs out to relieve themselves, then feed them, and let them out again a half hour later.
  • 8 am: Exercise and/or train each in turn.
  • 12 pm: Exercise all the dogs and allow them to relieve themselves.
  • 4 pm: Exercise all the dogs, allow them to relieve themselves, then feed.

• 6 pm: Exercise all the dogs and allow them to relieve themselves. This would also be a good time to take them all for a long walk in the woods or allow them to run in a safe field. Most dogs, especially when young, have a spurt of energy in the early evening.

• 9 pm: Exercise the dogs, feed them, and allow them to relieve themselves. Groom each one and do a body check with each. Then put them to bed for the night.

Daily walks provide your dogs with ample opportunity to eliminate and exercise.

You can vary this schedule which-ever way best suits you, but keep in mind that the dogs will need to know when they are going outside and when they are to be fed. Dogs that are maintained on a regular schedule are less likely to become overstressed.

Here is a schedule for someone who is away from home for up to nine hours a day:

• 6 am: Let the dogs outside to relieve themselves, feed them, and let them out again.

Before you leave for work, make sure that any young dogs are contained in a safe area where they cannot get into trouble. You can use a large crate, exercise pen, or, if your yard is fenced and the weather is nice, you can leave all the dogs outside. Make sure that they have shelter and water available during the day. The dogs will keep each other company during those long hours when you are away. If you need to confine your dogs inside, try to find a neighbor or teenager that can come over in the afternoons to let them out to play for a while and relieve themselves.

Many dog breeds have inherent abilities that can be worked into your exercise schedule. These Newfoundlands combine their love of water with a game of fetch with their owner.

• 6 pm: Greet your dogs and then feed them. If they had been contained indoors all day, take them outside first thing upon your arrival. Let them run and exercise.

• 8 pm: After you've eaten dinner and relaxed a little, take each dog in turn for some "alone" time. During this time you can groom the dog, train him, or just spend some time petting him. It's very important for each dog to have time alone with you.

Puppies will get easily distracted by any other dogs in the household, so be sure to keep them under careful supervision.

• 9-10 pm: Allow the dogs to relieve themselves and get a little exercise, do a body check, then put them to bed.

If one or both of your dogs are puppies, remember that they will eat slower and are more easily distracted than an adult dog. You'll also need to put aside more time to make sure your puppy does his business. While puppies often learn good potty habits from other dogs, there are some that are so distracted by the presence of their new siblings that they forget why they were let outside. If this is the case with your pup, then take him out separately and remain with him until he goes potty. This will have multiple benefits, because not only are you ensuring that the puppy learns where to do his business, but you are also bonding with him. Taking the time to bond with a new puppy is very important. You need to ensure that the pup learns that you are not only the leader of the pack, but also a source of love and nurture. Pups that grow up with only the company of other dogs often lose out on much needed human-canine socialization. Even though you may have gotten this new dog to keep your other dog company, it is of the utmost importance that you establish the same relationship with him as you did with dog number one.

Make sure that you spend ample time with each dog on an individual basis. Every dog in your home is entitled to the personal love and attention that you can give him.

Basic Training and Brace Training

T hose of us with two or more dogs may wonder where we'll get the time to go on more than one walk a day or practice training both of them. That's where brace work comes to play. The dogs will learn to work simultaneously off lead or eventually with no leash. This is also useful during everyday life. You don't want a pack of dogs racing through the door every time it's opened. Having them lined up in stays will ensure that they don't rush at visitors or jump all over the place when excited. You want dogs that come when called, regardless of what they're doing. Dogs that behave when together can go with you on any adventure.

When you have two dogs vying for top position in the pack, the best means of teaching them to live together is to teach them to work together first. Working side by side teaches them the most important lesson. ou are in charge. You choose which dog is higher or lower in the pack, and you decide who does what and when. Working them together satisfies their need to be with you at the same time. Not only are they by your side, but they are also using their mind and expending their

Before you can start training your dogs together, they must be able to perform all the basic commands separately.

Training classes are a great way to get started in basic obedience, as well as a good way to introduce your dog to other canines.

energy. After going through brace work, you'll see that the dogs are happier with each other and will tend to run and play side by side.

Before you can begin working the dogs together, you need to be sure that they can perform their basic commands as individuals. In fact, it's always a good idea to warm them up individually before working them together. Dogs often get so excited about being together that you'll have to first work on separating them before starting to teach them anything. The warm up will ensure faster cooperation.

BASIC TRAINING

Begin all training sessions by having your dog target on your hand. Targeting teaches your dog to watch your hand and to follow visual signals while listening to your vocal commands. You begin teaching the targeting exercise by placing a bit of food in your hand and letting your dog sniff it. When he does so, praise him and offer the treat. Before you know it, your dog is watching your hand with enthusiasm.

When both your dogs can walk on a leash and heel nicely, you can move on to more advanced leash training.

Begin teaching Scruffy to heel by putting your target hand under his nose. Arrange yourself so that Scruffy is on your left side. Hold the leash loosely in your right hand. Step forward on your left leg and say, "Scruffy, Heel." Go only three to five steps, then stop and say, "Scruffy, Sit." If Scruffy does not sit, put your target over his head and aim between his eyes. This makes him look up and puts his rear end down. As soon as Scruffy sits, give him the treat and lots of praise.

Each time you do the heel exercise, increase the amount of steps between each stop. If Scruffy does not move with you, slap your left leg and offer words of encouragement. Sometimes, there's a distraction that grabs his attention. Another noise or movement will return his attention to you, especially if you are holding something he really likes.

When you can heel for up to 20 steps, add turns into the routine. Right turns are a great means of correcting your dog for moving too far ahead of you. Left turns can be used to make Scruffy more aware of where you are and to watch you more attentively. The faster you do the turn, the more effectively it will teach Scruffy to pay attention. There's no need to repeat your command when you make a turn. Scruffy needs to learn to listen after you give only one command.

The stay command should be taught when your dog is reliably sitting on command. Begin by having your dog heel and sit. As soon as he sits, place the palm of your hand in front of his face, step out on your right leg directly in front of him, toe to toe, and say, "Scruffy, Stay." Remain only a couple seconds, return to the heel position, and give your dog his treat and lots of praise. If Scruffy moves out of his sitting position, replace him in the same spot and repeat your stay signal and command. Gradually, increase the amount of time Scruffy is to remain in that position. For example, begin by having him remain in place for five seconds. The next time, do the stay exercise for seven seconds, and so on.

Within a week or two, Scruffy should be able to maintain a sit/stay for a full minute. At this time, you can begin moving around him, increasing your distance while you do so. Keep in mind, however, that any increase in criterion should be done gradually. Begin moving around him by stepping side to side in front of him. When Scruffy remains still for this, walk along his sides. As your dog remains comfortable with this movement, go all the way around him. Remain close to him until you are able to walk around him several times in both directions. With this accomplished, gradually increase your distance as you move around him. For example, on the first sit/stay command, remain within one foot of him as you move around. The next time, move out to two feet, and so on, until you reach the end of your training leash.

The down command should be taught while you work on heeling. You should begin with your dog sitting at your side in heel position.

Once your dogs learn their obedience commands, they can go on to compete in organized dog sports like conformation, obedience, and agility.

The down command can be difficult for some dogs to accept because it puts them in a submissive position. These German Shepherds seem to have no problem.

Place the leash in your left hand as you give the down signal (pointing down in front of your dog's nose with your right forefinger). Be sure to say, "Scruffy, Down," in a very firm tone of voice.

If Scruffy does not lie down, and realistically, most dogs won't, put your left hand (with the leash still in it) on his shoulder blades. As you apply light pressure to his shoulder blades, put your right hand under his near foreleg, take hold of his far foreleg, and bring his forelegs forward as you press down.

As soon as Scruffy is down, offer him a treat and lots of praise. Maintain the light pressure on his shoulder blades and use your right hand to give the stay signal as you tell him, "Scruffy, Stay." Don't make him remain in this position for more than a few seconds. Quickly switch the leash over to your right hand (still maintaining the shoulder pressure with your left) and take him into a heel.

At this point in the training, try to begin varying the exercises. This is important because you don't want to pattern-train your dog. Dogs pick up on patterns very easily. So far, Scruffy has learned that every time you stop, he must sit. He may even have started doing this automatically, which is something you want. However, you don't want Scruffy to begin lying down every time you stop. Therefore, do not practice the down command more than two times in succession. When you stop, sometimes do a sit/stay and other times do a down/stay. You can even change things around more by either doing both or neither. Your dog can simply stop and sit, then go into a heel again.

The come command can be done from any position, even if your dog isn't working at the time. In fact, it's a good idea to practice calling Scruffy to come when he's playing. This teaches him to come to you at all times.

The come exercise is easiest to teach when working on a stay command. Simply go to the end of your training leash, bend forward at the waist, and say, "Scruffy, Come," in a happy tone of voice. As Scruffy comes to you, gather your leash so that it doesn't become caught up in his feet. When he arrives, stand upright, tell him to sit, and then give him a treat and lots of praise. Practice calling him from both in front, behind, and each side of him. If you are working him in the house, call him from behind a door or around a corner. Scruffy needs to learn to come to you whether you are in sight or not.

BRACE TRAINING

When brace training, you will need to use a tandem name for your dogs instead of their individual names so as not to confuse them. This way Scruffy and Fluffy won't think their names are Scruffyfluffy or Fluffyscruffy. A good tandem name should be very different from their individual names. A few suggestions are dogs, puppies, boys, or girls, or you can call them by breed: Springers, Shepherds, Collies, Pekes, Poodles, etc. This way, when you tell Scruffy to heel and Fluffy to stay, there won't be any misunderstanding.

Heeling in Brace

Begin by placing both dogs in sit/stays side by side. The slower dog should be on the inside (closer to your left leg) and the faster dog on the outside, shoulders even with the inside dog. Sometimes the speed of the dog does not designate its position. A dog that is more dominant may need to remain on the inside as the "preferred" position closest to you.

The first couple of times you try heeling in brace you will need to observe the dogs at work. If one keeps trying to nose into the inside position, you may want to keep the dog there from the start. However, if the inside dog tends to heel wide, forge ahead, or play too much with the outside dog, you should move his position to the outside.

Initially, you will be using two leashes so that you can control the two dogs individually. This may be confusing at first—after all, one leash was hard enough. (Wait until you're doing this with two long leashes. Talk about a handful!) Yes, it will be difficult to coordinate the leashes, especially consider- ing that you'll need to switch from a two-hand hold to a one-hand hold from time to time. Be pa- tient. Any time you get tangled, stop and put your dogs in a stay while you gather your leashes, (and wits) together.

The come command is one of the most important things you can teach your dogs, especially when you have more than one.

Position your dogs so that you get the optimum movement from each one. Penny, the dog closest to the handler, moves slower, while Emma, positioned on the outside, is faster.

Place the leash of the outside dog in your left hand and the leash of the inside dog in your right hand. Make sure the leash of your outside dog is behind the head of the inside dog. This will prevent the inside dog from biting at his leash or being pulled on by the outside dog's leash.

Due to the fact that you have to hold the leashes a little tighter and over the dog's heads, you cannot correct them for improper heeling in the same manner as when they worked individually. The only correction is to turn. Knowing which way to turn and when is part of the art of brace. For example:

Scenario #1: Both dogs are forging. Do a 90- or 180-degree turn to the right.

Scenario #2: The outside dog is forging. Do a 90-degree turn to the right.

Scenario #3: The inside dog is forging. Do a 90-degree turn to the left.

Scenario #4: The inside dog is being crowded out by the outside dog, causing the inside dog to lag. Do a 90-degree turn to the right as you urge the inside dog to catch up using a slap on the leg and encouraging vocal tones.

Scenario #5: Both dogs are lagging. Walk faster or do a slow jog as you use words of encouragement and slap your left leg.

Scenario #6: The dogs begin playing with one another. Don't stop and try to disentangle them. Keep moving quickly, doing turns and tugging the outside dog outward and the inside dog toward you, depending on which one is instigating the play.

All heeling corrections can be done through your turns. Therefore, you are to keep both leashes slack so that neither dog is getting dragged on at any time. As a rule, try to allow at least eight inches of leash between where your hand holds it and where the clip meets the head halter. Don't allow more than a foot and a half or your dogs will become entangled.

Before beginning brace training, initial heel work should be done with separate leashes until both dogs can work well together.

Sitting Together

Once you and your dogs have mastered the heel or at least gotten the rhythm, try stopping. You need to properly prepare for the stop in a fashion similar to when you initially worked Scruffy by himself. The leash should be gathered a little and glued to your thigh as you stop. Trying to use bait while working two dogs is next to impossible, unless you are able to hold it in your mouth and spit it at each dog in turn. Don't forget that with two dogs, that's twice as much bait, and unless you're a chipmunk, it can prove difficult. For this reason, you will need to guide your dogs into a sit by tightening your leashes before stopping.

Do not pull upward as you stop or as you tell them to sit. This is counterproductive to having the dogs learn to listen to commands and eventually work without a leash. Your

This Shih Tzu team learns to come and sit before their handler.

dogs should never be pulled into position at any time. Shortening the leashes simply allows you quicker access to the dog that doesn't stop quickly and sit.

Bring the leashes together as one and slide your left hand down them. Glue them to your thigh as you take that final step before stopping. With the shortened

These two hounds are being taught to work together while being trained with head halters.

leashes, your dogs won't be going anywhere. Because they've already been through basic training, they'll realize that stopping means they are to sit. If they do not do so automatically, you will need to use their tandem name and say, "Dogs, Sit."

If one dog sits and the other doesn't, then use the dog's individual name before your verbal reprimand and simultaneously pull upward under that dog's chin. The head halter will cause the dog's head to go up, making the rear end go down. If both dogs refuse to sit, then use your verbal reprimand and pull upward on both head halters until their rear ends touch the ground. This should not take more than a second or two. If they resist sitting, put a little pressure on their hips, each in turn. You don't want to keep their noses in the air with the head halters tight around their muzzles for any length of time. The correction should be

If one dog in your team breaks a command, he should be put back into position and the command should be repeated for that dog only.

quick and firm, and the release of pressure instantaneous.

If the outside dog sits too far away, try stopping with a fence to your left side, allowing just enough room for the dogs between you and that solid object. This way the dogs cannot turn out.

Sometimes, one of the dogs will stop too far in front of you. This can be a real trial. You will either have to physically move the dog back into position, which can be difficult, or do a finish. Sometimes you can avoid this by doing a left turn just before stopping. However, if this continues to occur, you will have to tell the dog that stopped in the proper spot to stay while you execute a finish with the other dog and guide him into the proper position.

The last thing you need is to allow your brace group to become sloppy. If at any time you need them to behave and be attentive, it's during brace work. Do what you have to in order to make sure that your dogs perform up to the same standards as when they work individually, but don't suddenly begin dragging them around. All procedures must be done in the same manner as when you worked them individually. This is the communication that Scruffy and Fluffy understand.

If the properly placed dog pops up while you are doing a finish with the other dog, then do a tandem finish. Place both leads into your right hand, step back on your right leg as you give the heel command, and perform the finish exactly as when you worked with them one on one. Once they are back in heel position, return the leashes into the appropriate hands—outside dog in your left hand, inside dog in your right hand.

Stay Together
The stay commands are probably the easiest thing to do in tandem. Since your dogs already know the meaning of stay, it's just a matter of acclimating them to performing it together.

Once you have them sitting or lying down, show them your visual cue and say, "Dogs, Stay." You only need to present your hand signal one time. There's no need to show each dog in turn. Step in front of them, right leg first. Gradually increase your distance as you walk around them.

If one pops up, say his name first and then the verbal reprimand as you replace him in his sit/stay. When both pop up, use only your verbal reprimand and replace them as close to where you originally put them as possible.

Doing tandem down/stays may be a little more difficult if one or both of the dogs aren't already going down on command. If you give the down command and they don't listen, you will need to place them into position before giving the stay command. The same holds true on the down/stay as with the sit/stay—if one doesn't listen, say the name before the verbal reprimand and placement. If both do not listen, use only the verbal reprimand and place them into their original place and position.

If the dogs are still trying to assert their position in the pack hierarchy, one or both may be reticent about lying down next to the other. The tandem down/stay is actually a great exercise in teaching them that you are alpha and, regardless of how they feel about each other, they must listen to you. This teaches them to get along with each other and relaxes them while together. Dogs are happiest when they know who is in charge—once they know, they readily follow their leaders and relax.

The Come

The come exercise is generally done in the same manner as when working with the dogs individually, only at this point, you have two leashes to gather simultaneously. Putting them together as one just before giving the come command will be helpful.

When working in brace, there are some major considerations to think of when doing the come exercise. Most importantly, you should not ask your dogs to come from behind them until they are working off lead and without a brace connector. Otherwise, you're asking for major entanglement and confusion. Do all come commands from in front of the dogs or from the sides, never from an area behind their bellies and definitely not from behind their tails.

Once trained on lead, both dogs can perform the same behaviors off lead. These Shih Tzu happily come to their owner, sit, and await their next command.

As you say, "Dogs, Come," bend at the waist. Just before they arrive, stand upright and give them the sit command. Both dogs should already be well versed in doing this exercise, but as with many situations, working in brace is a distraction in itself and one or both dogs may not readily respond. This is often solved when the brace connector is attached. One dog will complement the other on various exercises in which one of them might respond with style and the other poorly.

Due to the fact that you are using the leashes as one, whichever dog does not respond quickly will automatically receive a tug on his head halter.

As with the individual come exercise, both dogs should arrive in front of you and sit automatically. If one or both do not do so, do not

The connector you use will depend on the size and weight of your dogs. For smaller dogs, like Squeaky and Pip, use a shorter, lighter connector with a two-inch span on each side of the O-ring.

use any type of correction. Use the sit command first and if that does not work, place them into position. Never correct your dogs when they arrive. All come commands must remain as positive as possible.

Now that your dogs can work together in all their basic training and you have become a two-leash pro, it's time to use the brace connector.

The connector you use will depend on the size and weight of your dogs. Use a connector that is shorter and lighter in weight for smaller dogs, with a two-inch span on each side of the O-ring. Use the heavier nylon or leather connector with a four-inch span on each side of the O-ring for mid- to large-sized dogs.

Training your dogs together will help them to help each other. Each dog will try to emulate the other's good behavior.

Both dogs should wear their regular tag-bearing neck collars. You should never attach your dogs together using head halters or training collars. Clip the brace connector snaps to their regular neck collars. This way, if one dog listens and the other doesn't, the "bad" dog won't be pulled by his head or choked. He will only feel his regular collar, which won't have as much negative impact. The "bad" dog will be brought into position by the "good" dog with only a slight pull on his regular collar.

Training dogs together has another added benefit. It teaches a dog that does not respond quickly

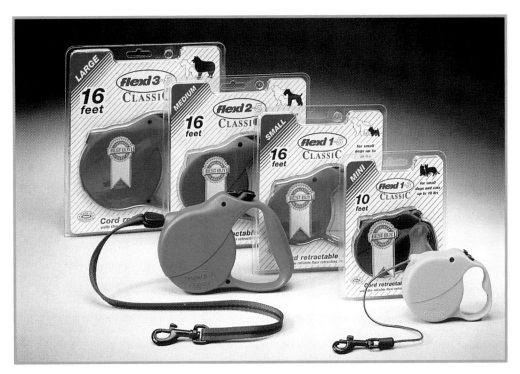

Retractable leashes provide dogs with freedom while allowing the owner to keep command at all times. Leashes are available in a wide variety of lengths for all breeds of dog. Photo courtesy of Flexi-USA, Inc.

to do so. Best of all, you are not the only one implementing the training. The "good" dog is also teaching the other dog.

This is a similar concept to ponying horses while training them. Ponying is used to teach a young horse the different gaits and turns, as well as to overcome fear of new places. Horses, being herd animals, prefer to remain close to other herd members. With ponying, they learn from each other in a comfortable manner. For example, a horse that is afraid to cross a creek is best taught by remaining close to another horse that isn't afraid. The frightened horse sees that his friend has no problem with the obstacle and will be more willing to accept the situation. Training in this manner is far more humane than trying to force a horse to cross the creek using whips and spurs. This method only teaches him that the creek is a bad experience, and most horses go out of their way to avoid a bad experience.

Dogs, as pack animals, prefer to remain in their "herd." Dogs learn a lot from each other. The brace work simply builds on this concept, and the dog that has the quicker response teaches the dog that has the slower response.

Initially, you'll continue to use the two leashes, until both dogs learn to work together and respond simultaneously. You'll have to help the more responsive dog teach the slower dog. When both dogs are working together with very little disruption, you can try putting one leash on the middle ring. It might be a good idea to attach short, lightweight leads to each dog's training collar just in case one dog becomes disruptive. If one of your dogs is young or easily distracted, you'll have far more control over the situation.

Once your dogs get the hang of working together, there is no limit to how far they can go.

MULTIPLE DOG HOUSEHOLDS

Play and Show

L iving with more than one dog offers hours of fun and laughs. Just watching the dogs play together can be entertaining. Play is healthy, both mentally and physically. Through daily play with your dogs, you bond and form relationships. This puts you in sync with the pack, and you will instantly know if there is a health or behavior problem, especially with an older dog. Not only does play promote the well-being of your dogs, it also helps your own mental state. How can you worry about the daily grind when your dogs are begging you to throw the ball or run through the woods? Coming home to dogs that greet you with enthusiasm and then want nothing other than to play with you has a way of clearing your mind.

There are both good and bad types of play. When living with more than one dog, you should monitor the games in order to prevent scuffles. You should also provide appropriate toys for your multi-dog household. There are some toys that might cause fights, especially treats. While these might be great for your dogs to chew on when you leave home for the day, they might begin stealing each other's toys (unless your dogs have been separated into crates or pens).

Playing with your dogs helps to keep them both physically and mentally healthy and creates a special bond between dogs and owner.

Some other great toys are fake lambskin teddy bears or other stuffed toys. However, if you have young children who like to play with stuffed animals, this should be avoided. Your dogs will think that the children's toys are fair game, too. In fact, you should never allow your dogs to chew on anything from your home that they *made* into a toy, such as old shoes, towels, socks, etc. Once they play with one of these items, they might think that the ones you care about are also toys.

Chewable bones or twisted rope toys can provide hours of fun for your dogs. Each dog can grab an end knot and play tug-of-war with each other. Although it's okay for your dogs to play tug-of-war, this is not a good game for you to become involved with. This game can often lead to an aggressive display or an accidental chomp on your hands. Besides, if you don't end it soon enough, your dog might begin thinking he is alpha. If you still wish to play this game, make sure

Playing fetch with your dogs is a great way to burn off their extra energy. These two Bearded Collies practice their soccer skills.

you first teach your dog the "drop-it" command. Every so often you should stop the game, have your dog sit, and tell him to drop the toy in your hand. This maintains your pack position.

Playing fetch is a great way of playing with more than one dog. You can use tennis balls, racquet balls, or Frisbees™. Be sure to have as many fetching objects as you do dogs. This will keep them playing with you instead of competing with each other. There are some breeds that enjoy playing with larger balls, such as soccer balls or basketballs. This can be loads of fun to watch as they tackle the balls or scoot the toys around with their noses.

Even though you may enjoy watching your dogs chase each other, it may not be a

Dogs will be dogs! It may seem as if your dogs play with each other in a rough manner, but unless one is really getting injured, don't interfere.

good idea for you to partake in this game if you have any children or senior citizens in your household. The last thing you want is for your dogs to run after and knock over moving children. Sometimes a chase game can get out of hand, and the dogs may jump all over you or nip at your heels. These are behaviors that need to be curbed, not enticed.

For dogs that are left alone for long periods of time, you may want to offer games that keep them occupied during their quiet time alone. Stuffing hollow toys with their kibble, peanut butter, or cheese will give them something to occupy their time and have fun with as they maintain a lower activity level. Putting ice cubes or apples in the water dish will keep them busy for a while as well.

A very constructive means of playing with your dogs is to teach them tricks. When all your dogs are obedience trained, you can place them in stays while working with one individual at a time. That way all the dogs are actually working, and you don't have to push one away while trying to teach another a new behavior.

Most dogs love to play with their Frisbees, and with a little practice, can even go on to compete in professional events.

All dogs love to learn tricks, such as shaking paws, rolling over, and begging. Many will anxiously look forward to these training sessions, often going to their training spots with grins on their faces. You can fit a trick here and there into your normal training routine. Have your dogs perform a trick before you leave in the morning or just before bedtime. You'll get as much joy out of watching all your dogs do simultaneous tricks as they will have in performing them.

SHAKE

Begin with your dog in the sit/stay. Hold a treat in your left hand and let your dog

Teaching your dogs to perform tricks is a very constructive way of playing. Not only is this dog learning to shake hands, he is expanding his training knowledge.

target on it. As soon as he puts his nose on your hand, praise him and give him the treat. The next time you offer your target hand, bring your dog's head toward his right side. As he shifts his weight to the right, he will take the weight off his left foreleg. Say, "Scruffy, Shake," and tap the foreleg with your right hand. When he lifts the paw, praise him and give the treat. Each time you do the exercise, do not give the treat until Scruffy lifts the paw a little higher. Before long you'll have his paw in your hand doing the shake trick.

ROLL OVER

Begin with your dog in a down/stay. While he remains down, have your dog target on your hand as you

This Australian Shepherd learns how to beg on command by following his owner's hand signals.

bring it toward his hip. Tell him, "Scruffy, Roll Over." Scruffy will shift his weight to the other side as he reaches for the target. When he does so, give him praise and the treat. Next time, make him reach a little farther so that he rolls partially onto his back. Each time, ask for a little more movement so that eventually he is totally lying on his back. Some dogs may need your help to make it completely over. Gently take their hind legs and move them around. As soon as they reach the other side, praise and give the treat. Many dogs will quickly catch on as their target continues to make the circle around their tummies and to their other side. Praise as they move, but don't give the treat until they have made the complete circle.

BEG

You may want to begin this trick by making sure you have your dog doing a sit/stay in a corner. A corner will offer back support when he rises up. This is especially important when teaching this trick to a puppy or elderly dog. Falling over backward can be detrimental to their bodies, as well as discouraging when trying to learn a new trick.

Put your target hand a few inches above your dog's nose and point upward with the index finger of the target hand. Say, "Scruffy, Beg." Your dog will look up and try to touch his nose against your hand. When he does, praise him and give him the treat.

Next time as he raises his nose, lift your hand a little higher (never more than a couple inches from his nose) as he stretches to reach the target. Again, give him the command and offer praise and reward when he goes up a little higher. Each time you do the exercise, ask for a little more lift off the ground.

Some dogs have very poor balance and offering them your other hand to rest a paw upon might be helpful in building their confidence. As they learn how to balance on their hind end, you can reduce the amount of weight you allow on your hand. Always praise and reward each little increment.

TRICKS TOGETHER

When you teach more than one dog to do tricks, you've made your own circus act. You can teach them to do everything simultaneously. Line them all up in a sit/stay when asking for the shake or beg and in a down/stay for the roll over.

When doing the shake, ask each in turn to lift their paws. Reward them all at the same time when each has done the behavior. Do the same for when they beg. Within a few weeks, you'll only need to give one signal and command for all of them to perform at the same time.

The roll over is a little more complicated. You'll have to ask each dog in turn, or they'll be rolling over each other, making it difficult for each to perform. Place the dominant dog at the end of the row and request the trick from him first. As soon as he rolls over, make him continue to remain in the down/stay. Then ask the next dog to roll over, and on down the line. Once all the dogs have completed the roll over and are still in their down/stays, release them and give them their treats. Always keep in mind that the alpha dog should receive the first treat and work your way down the hierarchy, with the omega dog receiving his treat last.

There are loads of activities you can do with more than one well-trained dog. A hike in the mountains, a swim in a lake, or a game of ball in a field are but a few. There are also competitive sports, such as obedience trials, agility, flyball, and much more. You can teach your dogs how to be therapy pals for the injured, sick, or elderly. The possibilities are endless.

OBEDIENCE COMPETITION

There are many levels of obedience competition and several ways to compete. The American Kennel Club (AKC) offers trials for purebred dogs, while the United Kennel Club (UKC) will allow mixed breeds to compete as well. Each club has their own set of rules and guidelines, which can be obtained when you contact them.

The AKC hosts three levels of competition with advanced certificates for earning a specific amount of points. The levels are Novice (Companion Dog, CD), Open (Companion Dog Excellent, CDX) and Utility (Utility Dog, UD). The advanced certificates include Utility Dog Excellent (UDX) and Obedience Trial Champion (OTCh.).

For those who have more than one purebred dog, the AKC offers a class called Brace. In this class, two dogs compete simultaneously, working through the Novice level guidelines. Both dogs must do the following exercises.

First, they must work at the handler's left side, wearing a brace connector and one leash attached between them. They must perform a heeling pattern, which includes several stops, 90-degree turns, 180-degree turns, and changes of pace. Then they perform the heel around two people standing eight feet apart. This is called

This chorus line of canines is learning to speak on cue.

Competing in obedience competition is a great way to further your dog's training and can be a fun experience for both you and your dog.

the figure-eight exercise. Next, they must stand for examination, and both dogs must stand side to side, off leash, while the judge touches their heads, shoulders, and backs. Once completed, they must perform the off-leash heel pattern, which is usually similar to the on-lead pattern. The last individual exercise is the recall. Both dogs are left in sit/stays at one end of the ring, and the handler goes to the other end. Upon a signal from the judge, the handler calls the dogs to come and sit facing him/her. The individual exercises are completed with a finish, in which the dogs return to heeling position, either by passing behind the handler's back or walking down the person's left side and turning to sit in heel position.

Besides both dogs performing as requested and being braced together, they must try to remain side to side as much as possible throughout the exercises. This means that an inside dog, the one closest to the handler, may have to walk more slowly around corners, while the outside dog must move more quickly.

If you are competing in classes where you can only enter one dog at a time, such as a conformation class or one of the regular levels of obedience, either have someone help you hold the other dog(s) or bring along crates and pens for containment. The last thing you want to see is your other dog running loose through the show grounds while you're in the ring competing.

When showing more than one dog, it would be wise to make a list of things you will need to keep your dogs and yourself comfortable. This list should include pens and crates, water and water dishes, a ground rug to keep the dogs from becoming dirty, and a tent or sun reflector to keep the dogs cool. There are also portable fans to maintain your dogs body temperature on a hot day and you should bring grooming brushes, dry shampoo, and towels with you. If you are planning an overnight excursion, remember to pack your dogs' normal diets and a large jug of water from home. When packing for yourself, add a folding chair or two, a table, a cooler with drinks, reading material for those long waits between classes, and pictures of your brood to show off to all the other dog enthusiasts. These are people who can truly appreciate your obsession with having more than one dog.

AGILITY

If obedience trials are too tame for your tastes, try agility. Modeled after the equestrian stadium jumping, agility is growing in popularity throughout the nation. Dogs must traverse and jump obstacles in a specific order while being timed. These obstacles include an A-frame; a dog walk, which is an elevated narrow plank; a see-saw; weaving poles; a tire jump; various bar, high, and broad jumps; a pipe tunnel; a collapsed tunnel; and a pause table, in which the dog must jump onto a platform and remain there for a set period of time.

Throughout the trial, handlers cannot touch or bait their dogs, only tell them which obstacle to do next. Therefore, as your dog learns to traverse an obstacle, he must also learn the name of it. Each trial has a different course and level of difficulty. In the advanced levels, obstacles are often put in the path of the competitors that are not to be the next in line for the set course.

Due to the large variety of dog breeds, agility trials offer specific divisions according to size. This also helps with setting the jump heights at appropriate levels. After all, it wouldn't be fair to ask a Corgi to jump as high as a Border Collie.

There are three main levels in the AKC's agility trials. Novice class presents 12 to 13 obstacles. The dog must travel two yards per second, with five seconds on the pause table. In Open class, 15 to 17 obstacles are presented. The dogs in the 8- to 12-inch divisions must travel 2 and one-fourth yards per second, with 5 seconds for the pause table. Those dogs in the 16-inch division must travel almost 2 and one-half yards per second, with 5 seconds on the pause table. Dogs in the 20- and 24-inch division must travel 2 and one-half yards per second, with an additional 5 seconds on the pause table. The Excellent class has 18 to 20 obstacles. The 8- to 12-inch-high dogs must travel at 2 and one-half yards per second. The 16-inch-high dogs must travel at 2 and three-quarters yards per second, and the 20- to 24-inch dogs must go 3 yards per second. All dogs must still wait five seconds on the pause table.

Agility is an action-packed sport that is exciting for everyone involved, including the dogs, handlers, and spectators.

Some breeds have the inherent urge to retrieve and will happily participate in any event or game that includes this activity.

Dogs are judged on their ability to traverse the course in the allotted period of time and on their performance over the obstacles. Dogs that refuse an obstacle are given major penalties, and those that exceed the maximum course time are excused from the ring. Excessive handling or harsh reprimands are also a cause for disqualification.

To participate in agility, Scruffy must be well-trained off lead and distraction proofed. He must have athletic ability and the desire to perform. Playing retrieving and find-it games from the time your dog is a puppy is also helpful. These teach him to think and reason. They also teach him to traverse obstacles, even if they are as simple as a couch or a lawn chair.

Begin agility training by teaching Scruffy to traverse low or smaller versions of the obstacles. Hurdle training is very helpful in preparing for agility. When teaching Scruffy to go over the see-saw, A-frame, or dog walk, you should physically guide him by placing a treat or toy before his nose with one hand and guiding his body with your other hand. This helps him gain confidence, especially on the wobbly see-saw. Using bait will also help Scruffy through the pipe and collapsed tunnels. Having Scruffy do a stay on the pause table prepares him for his automatic five-second hesitation during a performance.

Once Scruffy understands each of the obstacles, you can gradually condition him to the jump heights he'll have to eventually traverse in competition. Scruffy will also need to learn these commands—slow, fast, turn left or right, and to move away or closer to his handler.

TRACK AND FIELD

Tracking and field work allow your dogs to use their natural hunting abilities. The AKC offers three levels of tracking tests. The basic test, which when completed gives the dog a TD (Tracking Dog) title, consists of a track that is approximately 440 and 500 yards long. The track is laid between 30 minutes and 2 hours prior to the dog's performance. Included are three to five left and right turns. The surface for this basic test is generally the same, such as all grass without any water or paved road. To earn the TD title, the dog must also find an article, such as a glove or wallet.

The next level is the Tracking Dog Excellent (TDX) test. This differs from the first test in that the dog will have to deal with obstacles on his track, such as a fence or wall. The dog will also have to cross track and find four articles. Various types of terrain, such as woods, vegetation, streams, and gullies, will also have to be traversed.

The Variable Surface Tracking (VST) test will be anywhere from 600 to 800 yards in length. The dog will have to track through a minimum of three different surfaces, such as asphalt, mulch, gravel, or concrete. There will also be four to eight turns, some of them right angle turns. The dog will have to locate four articles that are everyday items, such as a leather wallet, a plastic bottle, a piece of cloth or something made of metal.

Tracking may sound difficult, but your dogs will thoroughly enjoy it well into their senior years. In fact, many dogs that can no longer compete in an activity that requires jumping can still perform the job that utilize their natural gifts. A dog's nose is an incredible biological attribute, allowing them to not only discern individuals, but to know when they were at a specific spot and their state of mind when they were there.

Dogs can scent track in a variety of ways, making them a great complement to our society. Not only can they find scent on an object or on the ground, but also in the air. This allows them to help us find lost children, discover hidden narcotics and weapons, or track down criminals. Teaching your dogs to track is a gift to them, and you'll have a great time, too.

Field training is also fun for your dogs, especially if they are sporting dogs. This, too, makes use of the abilities specifically bred into them. Again, your dogs will

Tracking events allow your dogs to use their natural scenting abilities in the show ring. These Beagles work a rabbit track at a field trial.

have to first complete on- and off-lead obedience training, as well as become very adept at retrieving. They must also be able to contain themselves and retrieve only when directed to do so and not whenever they see the "duck" go down. This is important, because at a field event, several dogs are lined up waiting for their turns, as the dogs in front of them are sent to retrieve. Moreover, a dog must be patient off lead, without his handler holding him in any manner.

When ordered to retrieve, the dog must quickly search out the "duck," whether on land or in the water, and smartly bring it back to his handler. He must also deliver the "duck" with a soft mouth so as not to bruise the game. The handler can give him direction signals, such as right or left. The dog mustn't overly disturb the ground throughout his search and retrieve.

Dogs that return without the "duck" or don't listen to their handlers are considered out of control and eliminated from the competition. Also, dogs that mangle their "duck" will be excused from the trial. To make this even more difficult, there are decoys placed within the area and if the dog retrieves a decoy instead, he will be eliminated.

Field trials are most enjoyed by those who like to hunt with their dogs. The competition gets them out in the country and allows their dogs a chance to run as they were meant to do. If you live in an urban area with your sporting dogs, you may want to look into field work as a means of getting into the country on weekends. It'll be great exercise for all of you.

Flyball is a great way for you and your dogs to perform as a team, get plenty of exercise, and make new friends.

There are plenty of activities for you to participate in with your dogs. As long as you treat them as part of the family, they will be happy to accompany you anywhere.

FLYBALL

Flyball is another way of getting both exercise and finding new friends. This sport also requires that your dogs have off-lead training and work well with distractions—and there are plenty of distractions at a flyball tournament. A flyball competition is essentially a relay race, with four people and dogs per team. The dogs are sent to the opposite end of their lane, jump on a flyball box to release the tennis ball, and then return the ball to their handler before the next dog can take a turn. The dogs must remain in their own lanes and not retrieve fallen balls in the next lane over, which is a tough request. Distraction proofing is a must. The first team to have all their dogs run through the course wins. The more advanced tournaments include a series of four jumps in which the dogs must go over both on the way to the flyball box and back.

This is a guaranteed good time, both for competitors and observers. You can also bet that the dogs enjoy it.

Although there are many organized activities offered by kennel clubs, there is plenty that you and your dogs can do without having to compete. You can go hiking, camping, traveling, and more. Don't limit yourself only to what's around you. Let your imagination fly. Stimulation is the key to good health and well-being. Keep finding new things to do and places to go.

When one of your dogs can no longer keep up with vigorous adventures, try something else, such as teaching him to be a therapy dog. Not only will the residents of hospitals and nursing homes love to see him, he'll adore all the attention and fuss. Let the younger dogs catch the balls and allow your older dog to enjoy the spoils of seniority—lots of love.

Resources

1.

    Flexi USA, Inc.
    147 Circle Freeway
    Cincinnati, Ohio 45246
    www.flexiusa.com
    flexiusa@flexiusa.com

    Flexi retractable leashes are the original retractables. Flexi, made in Germany, is the worldwide market leader and the only manufacturer with a large selection of models and retractable leashes to fulfill the needs of all breed sizes.

2.

    American Kennel Club
    260 Madison Avenue
    New York, New York 10016
    or 5580 Centerview Drive
    Raleigh, North Carolina 27606
    919-233-3600
    919-233-9767
    www.akc.org

3.

    The Kennel Club
    1 Clarges Street
    Picadilly, London WIY 8AB, England

4.

    Canadian Kennel Club
    100-89 Skyway Avenue
    Etobicoke, Ontarion, Canada M9W6R4